W9-BXD-168

"Your word is like a lamp that shows me the way. It is like a light that guides me."

–Psalm 119:105 (NIrV)

Presented to:

From:

Date:

ZONDERKIDZ

Read with Me Bible for Toddlers
Text Copyright © 2009 by Zondervan
Illustrations Copyright © 2005 by Dennis G. Jones

Requests for information should be addressed to:
Zonderkidz, Grand Rapids, Michigan 49530

Library of Congress Cataloging-in-Publication Data

Read with Me Bible for Toddlers / written by Doris Wynbeek Rikkers; illustrated by
Dennis G. Jones.
    p. cm.
    ISBN 978-0310-71877-2 (hardcover)
1. Bible stories, English. I. Jones, Dennis G., 1956- II. Title. BS551.3.R54 2009
220.9'505
[E]--dc22

2008051570

Published in association with the literary agency of Alive
Communications, Inc., 7680 Goddard Street #200,
Colorado Springs, CO 80920. www.alivecommunications.com

Editorial Direction: Doris Rikkers
Art Direction & Interior Composition: Cindy Davis

Zonderkidz is a trademark of Zondervan.

Printed in China

09 10 11 12 • 10 9 8 7 6 5 4 3 2 1

Read with Me Bible

for toddlers

Written by **Doris Wynbeek Rikkers**

Illustrated by **Dennis G. Jones**

ZONDERkidz

ZONDERVAN.com/
AUTHORTRACKER
follow your favorite authors

OLD TESTAMENT

The Very Beginning

Genesis 1–2:3

In the beginning, there was nothing.

The dark was everywhere.

On day one
God said, "Light, shine!"

Jesus disappeared behind a cloud into heaven.
An angel came and said to the disciples, "Why are you looking
at the sky? Jesus will come back again someday."

And the light came out of the dark.
God called the light "day." He called the dark "night."

On day two
God said, "Water above, separate from the water below."

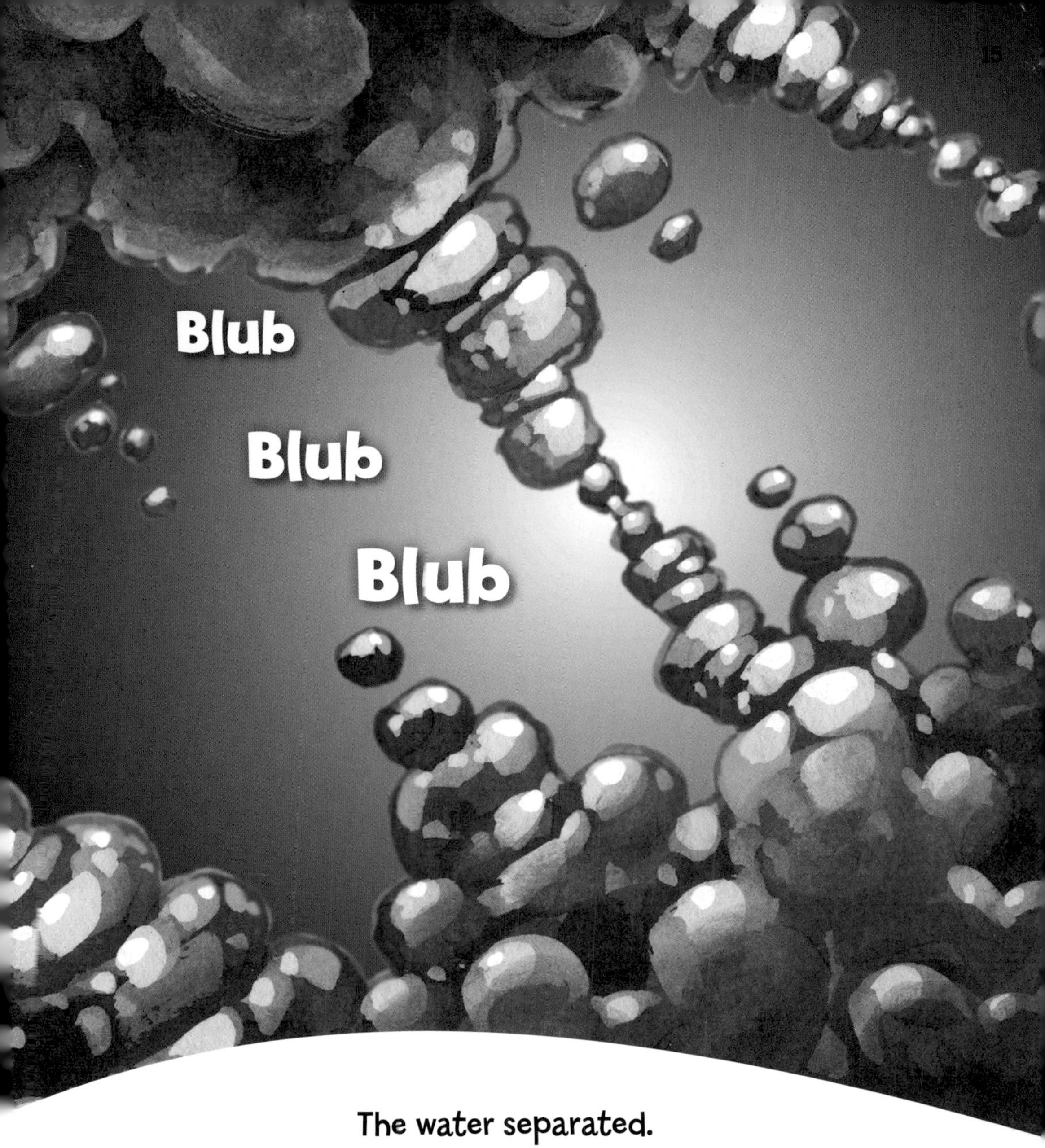

Blub

Blub

Blub

The water separated.
God called the new space "sky."

On day three
God said, "Water, crowd together so some places are dry."
God called the water "sea."

He called the dry land "earth."
Then plants, trees, and flowers popped up
and covered the earth.

On day four

God said, "Sun, shine during the day."

"Moon and stars, shine at night."
And they did.

On day five
God said, "Fish, swim in the sea. Birds, fly in the sky."
And they did.

On day six
God said, "Animals, jump and run. Swing from the trees.
Slop in the mud." And they did.

God created a man named Adam to take
care of the plants and animals.
God made a woman named Eve to be a friend to Adam.

On day seven
God rested. Everything was perfect. Everyone was happy.

Adam and Eve Sin

Genesis 2-3

Adam and Eve were happy. They lived in the garden of Eden.

God told them, "You can eat any fruit you
find in the garden. But don't eat the fruit from
the tree in the middle of the garden."
Adam and Eve did what God said.

But a clever, sneaky snake said to Eve, "Go ahead.
Eat that fruit too."

"No, I can't," said Eve. "God told us not to."

"Sure you can," said the snake.

"Well, maybe I could," said Eve. "That fruit sure looks tasty."

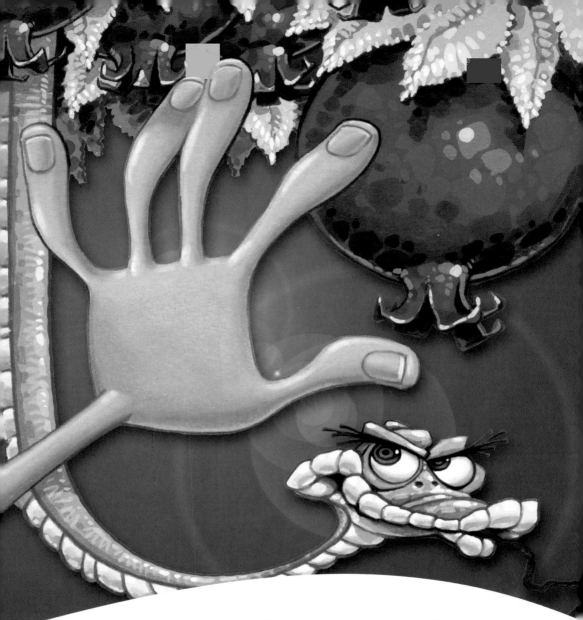

Eve reached up. She picked a piece of fruit.

Eve took a bite. **Yummmmmm.**

Eve shared the fruit with Adam.
They both ate the fruit God told them *not* to eat.

Suddenly they knew they had done something very, very wrong. They had disobeyed God.

God made them leave the beautiful garden.

Noah Builds an Ark

Genesis 6–9

God told Noah to build an ark, a big boat—so big
that it could hold two of every kind of animal in
the world, plus Noah and his family.

"I'm going to flood the earth with water," God said.
"But you will be safe inside the boat."

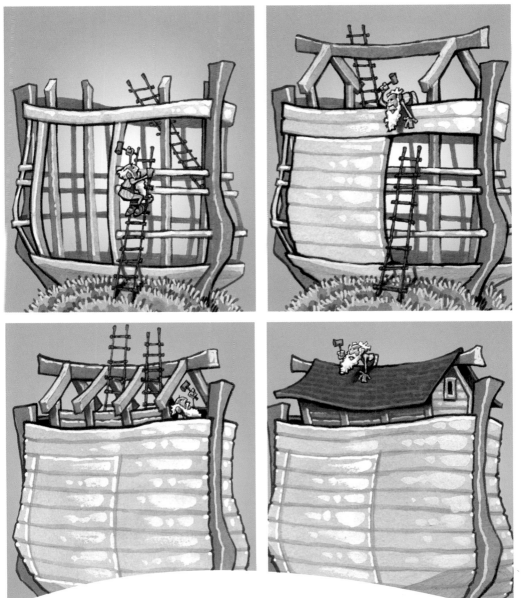

Noah warned his neighbors about the flood.
They laughed at him. But Noah kept building
the boat—day after day until it was finished.

"March the animals two by two into the boat," God told Noah.

All the animals hurried to get a place on Noah's boat.

"This way," Noah called to the animals.
Animals from all over the world scampered and scurried,
hopped and trotted, crawled and flew into the boat.

The clouds burst open, and rain poured down.
The water got deeper and deeper and deeper.
Soon Noah's boat was floating on the waves.

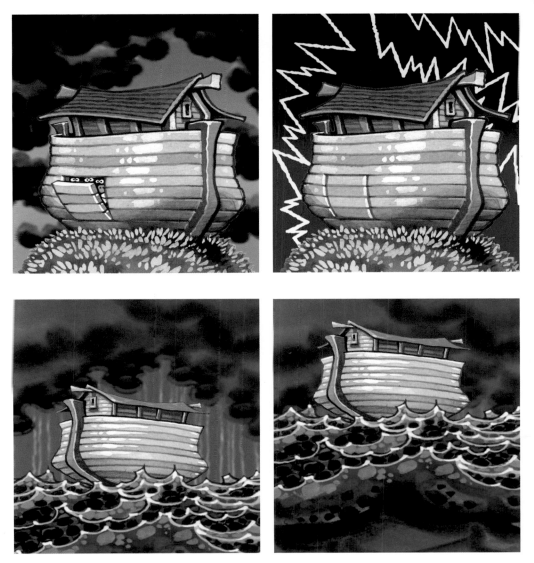

The last two animals climbed on board.
God closed the door.
The sky got dark. The thunder ROARED.

Noah and all the animals were safe and warm
and happy inside the big boat.

After many, many days of rain, the storm stopped.
The sun came out, and dry land appeared.
Noah sent out a dove, and it came back
with an olive branch in its beak.

God told Noah it was safe to leave the ark.
The animals ran out the door and danced on the ground.
God saved them all from the terrible flood.

Moses Leads the Israelites

Exodus 2–12

One day the princess of Egypt spotted a basket floating in the river.
"Oh, look," she said. "There's a baby in the basket!"
She carried the baby home and named him Moses.

The princess loved the baby Moses and
raised him as her own son.

Moses grew up in the palace of the pharaoh.
He dressed like a royal prince.

One day Moses was very, very angry, and he left Egypt.
He ran away to the desert and took care of sheep.

Many years passed. Moses was old.
He was on Mount Sinai when he saw something strange.
A bush was on fire. He went over to take a closer look.

Then God's voice came out of the burning bush. "Moses," God said. "My people are still in Egypt. They need your help. Go back to Egypt and get them away from Pharaoh."

Moses returned to Egypt.

"Pharaoh," he said.
"God wants his people
to be free. Let the
Hebrew people go into the
desert to worship their God.
If you don't do what God says,
terrible things will happen."

"All the water in Egypt will turn to blood.

Frogs will jump on everything.

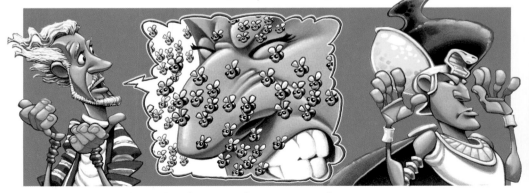

Gnats will bite people and crawl up your nose.

Flies will fill your house and cover the ground.

Your cows and camels, sheep and goats, horses and donkeys will die.

Boils will pop out on people and animals."

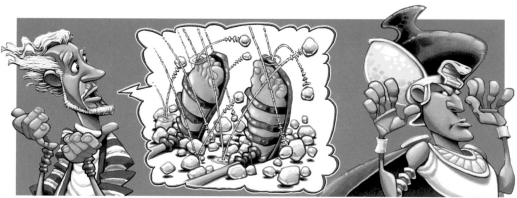

"Hailstones will knock you down and smash trees.

Grasshoppers will cover the land and eat your crops.

Darkness will be everywhere for three full days."

God sent the plagues like Moses said. But Pharaoh would not let the people go. Then God sent the tenth plague and the oldest son in every Egyptian family died. Pharaoh's son died too.

"Can we leave NOW?" asked Moses.
"Just GO," Pharaoh said.

After many, many years, God's people left Egypt.
They were eager to go to the new land God promised them.

The Great Escape

Exodus 14

Moses led God's people out of Egypt.
They traveled in the desert until they came to the
shore of the Red Sea.

"Now what do we do?" the people asked.

The people heard a RUMBLE and ROAR.
They turned around and saw the army
from Egypt charging toward them!

"Oh God," Moses prayed. "Please help us.
Our enemy is behind us, and the sea is in front of us.
We can't move."

"Raise your staff over the water and
watch what I do," God said.

Moses raised his staff over the water.

Suddenly a mighty wind blew across the sea.
The waves piled up on the left and on the right,
leaving a dry path in the middle of the sea.

God's people hurried across the dry path through the sea.
"Go after them!" commanded the leader of the army.

All the chariots, horses, and soldiers charged
after the people as they ran to the other side.

When God's people were safe on the other side of the sea,
Moses raised his staff again. The walls of water
crashed down and washed away Pharaoh's army.

"Hurray," shouted the people.
"We are free! God saved us from our enemy."

40 Years in the Desert

Exodus-Numbers-Deuteronomy

God took care of his people in the desert.
He gave them manna and quail to eat.
He gave them water to drink.

God gave the people the Ten Commandments—rules to
live a happy life. He saved them from poisonous snakes.
God divided the Jordan River so the people could cross into
the Promised Land.

Joshua and the Battle of Jericho

Joshua 6

God's people were excited. They crossed the Jordan River
and entered the land God had promised them.
But first they had to conquer the city of Jericho. The city was
big. Strong, stone walls surrounded it.

God told Joshua what to do. "Don't be afraid. I will help you. March the soldiers around the city one time every day for six days. Tell the priests to carry the ark of the covenant and march with you. On the seventh day, march around the city seven times. Then watch what happens!"

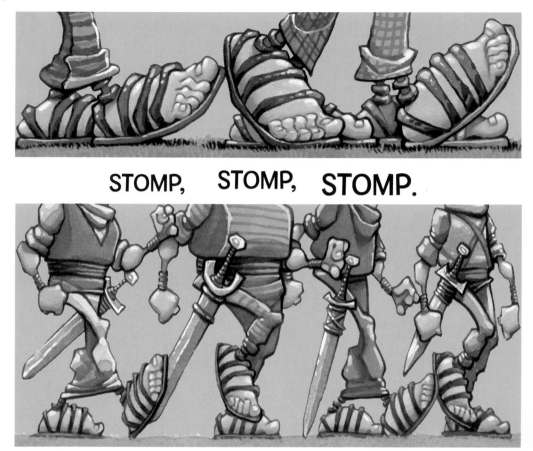

STOMP, STOMP, STOMP.

TROMP,
TROMP,
TROMP.

Joshua marched the soldiers around the city every day for six days. On the seventh day, they marched around seven times and stopped. Then the priests blew their horns, the people shouted and ...

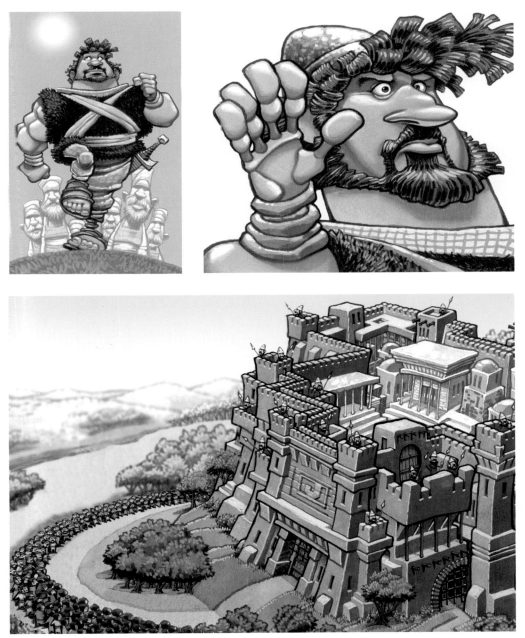

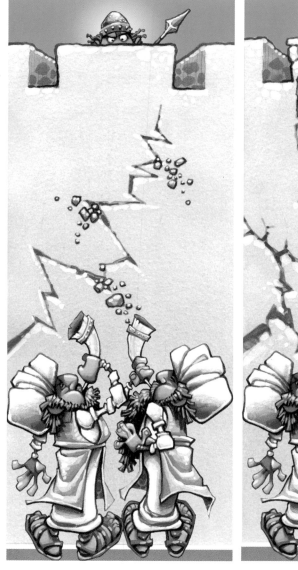

RUMBLE,   RUMBLE,

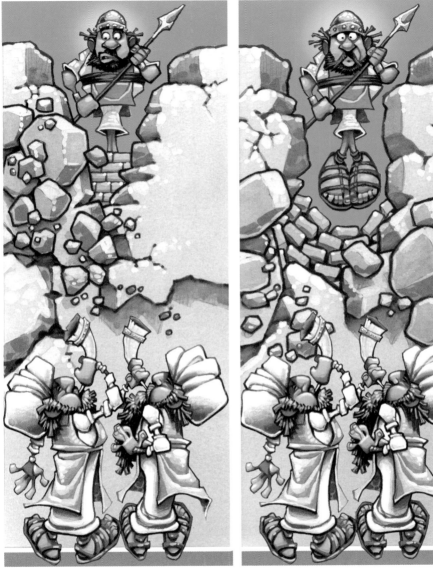

CRA-A-A-CK,

TUMBLE!

The walls of Jericho fell down!
The people shouted with joy, "WE WON!
God helped us conquer the city of Jericho!"

David Fights Goliath

1 Samuel 17

God's people were afraid.
A giant named Goliath wanted to fight one of their soldiers.

"WHO WILL FIGHT ME?" shouted Goliath.

A small boy named David carried bread and cheese
to his brothers. He heard the giant shout.

"You know," David said, "I could fight this giant. God will help me."

David went to the king.
"I am strong," said David. "I will fight the giant for you."

"I fought a lion. I killed a bear. I can handle Goliath."

The king agreed to let David fight the giant. He gave
David a sword. He put a heavy helmet on his head.
But David could not move.

David took off all the protective armor and walked away.

David stopped at a babbling brook
and prayed to God for help.

He picked up five smooth stones and
put them in his pouch.

David confidently marched up the hill to face Goliath.
Goliath growled and snarled at him.

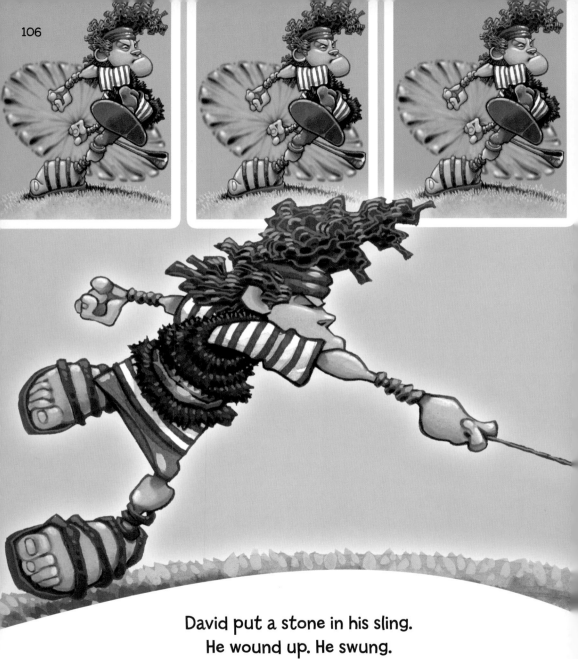

David put a stone in his sling.
He wound up. He swung.
The stone flew and ...

WHACK!
The stone hit Goliath in the head.

Goliath crashed to the ground.
Little David conquered the giant with God's help.

Daniel and the Lions

Daniel 6

Daniel lived in a far away land. He prayed to God every day.
The king of Babylon did not know Daniel's God.
He made a rule that no one could pray.

When the king walked by, everyone bowed down to him.
But Daniel did not.

Instead, Daniel went to his room.
He knelt down and prayed to God.
Daniel gave thanks to God three times a day.

The king's men arrested Daniel because
he broke the new rule.

The guards threw Daniel into a pit full of hungry lions.

Daniel prayed to God for help. God sent an angel to protect Daniel. The angel closed the mouths of the lions.

All night long the angel kept the lions away from Daniel.
The next morning the king called to Daniel.
"Daniel, has your God saved you?"
"Yes," Daniel answered. "God sent an angel to close
the mouths of the lions. They didn't hurt me at all."

The king was happy. He took Daniel out of the lion's den.
He told everyone in the kingdom that God had saved Daniel.

Jonah and the Big Fish

Jonah 1-3

Jonah was God's prophet. Jonah told the people of Israel what God was planning to do.

"Jonah," God called, "go to the city of Nineveh. You must tell the people there to stop doing bad things and believe in me."

Jonah did not want to go to Nineveh.
He did not want to do what God said.

Jonah wanted to run away from God. He climbed aboard
a boat that was going to the city of Tarshish.

The sea was calm when the boat left. Then God sent a powerful storm. The wind blew. The waves crashed over the boat. The sailors were afraid. They screamed at Jonah, "WAKE UP!"

"How can you sleep? We are scared.
Get up and pray to your God to save us!"

The sailors asked Jonah, "Who are you? Where did you come from? Why is this storm here?"
Jonah said, "It's my fault. I'm running away from God. Throw me overboard, and the storm will stop."

The sailors threw Jonah overboard, and the sea became calm.

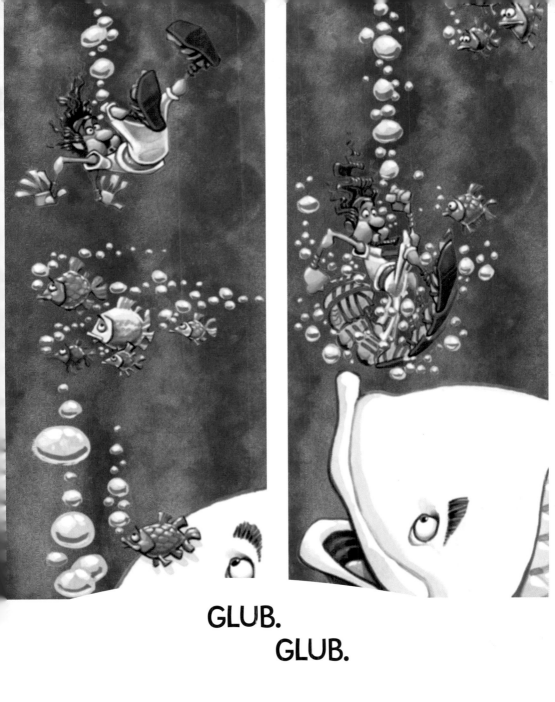

GLUB.
GLUB.

God sent a huge fish to catch Jonah.
GULP!

Jonah was stuck inside the stomach of the fish
for three days and three nights.

Jonah prayed to God for help.

God spoke to the fish. The fish spit out Jonah.
PITUUEEE!

Jonah went flying through the air,
head over heels and onto the shore.

God spoke to Jonah a second time, "Jonah, go to Nineveh."
Jonah obeyed God this time. He went to Nineveh. He preached to
the people about God. The people of Nineveh believed what Jonah
said. They were sorry about the bad things they had done.

NEW
TESTAMENT

Jesus Is Born

Luke 2; Matthew 2

Stars twinkled in the midnight sky.
Everything was quiet. Everyone was asleep.

Mary, Joseph, and their donkey had traveled all day to get to Bethlehem. They needed a place to sleep.

Joseph knocked on a door. "You can't stay here.
My inn is full," the innkeeper said.

Joseph went to another inn and knocked.
"No, no," the innkeeper said. "We have no room for you here."

Joseph knocked on another door.
"Hmm. I don't have room for you in my house," the man said.

"But you can use the place out back."

The innkeeper showed Joseph and Mary the stable.
"You can sleep out here," he said. "The goats and
cows and chickens won't mind."

During the night, Mary gave birth to a baby boy.
She named him Jesus.

Outside the town of Bethlehem, the shepherds were dozing around their campfire.

Suddenly angels appeared in the sky!
"Yikes!" the shepherds shouted.

"Don't be afraid," the angel said. "I've got good news!
A baby was born in Bethlehem—his name is Jesus.
He will save the world from sin."

"Go to Bethlehem. You will find a baby in a manger.
Go and see."

The shepherds hurried into the city.
They found Mary and Joseph and the baby Jesus,
just like the angel said.

Jesus grew ... and **grew** ... and **grew**.

While Jesus grew, wise men traveled from a far away land.
They saw a special star in the sky and
followed it to where Jesus lived.

The wise men gave Jesus special gifts.
They bowed down and worshipped him.

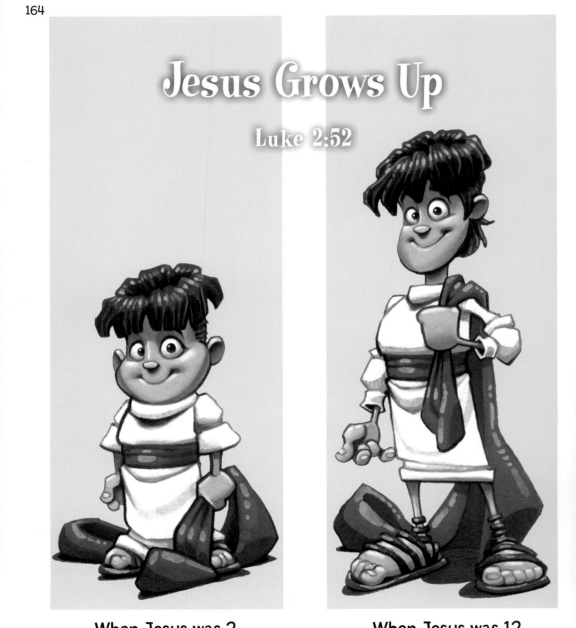

Jesus Grows Up

Luke 2:52

When Jesus was 2,
the wise men came.

When Jesus was 12,
he went to the temple.

When Jesus was 20,
he was a carpenter.

When Jesus was 30,
he began to preach.

Jesus grew up, like all children do.

John the Baptist

Mark 1

John the Baptist was a preacher. He wore clothes made from camel's hair. When people told him they were sorry for their sins, John baptized them in the Jordan River.

Jesus came to the river.
"John, I would like you to baptize me," he said.

Jesus walked into the river.
John baptized Jesus in the water.

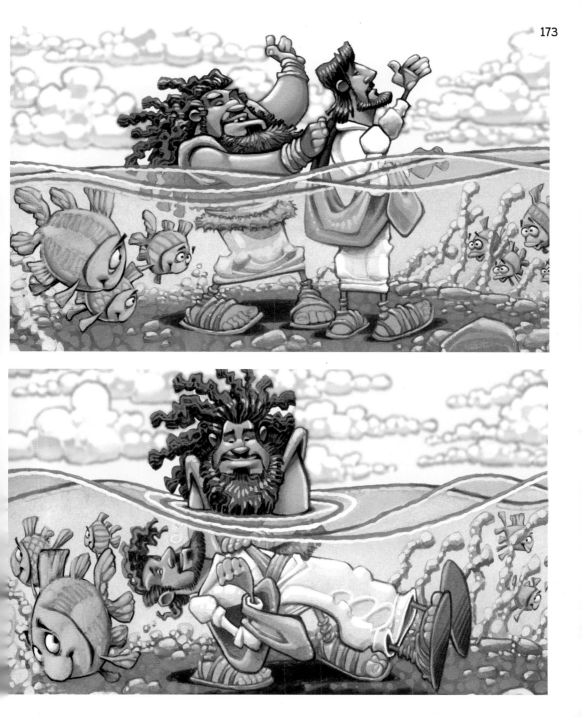

As Jesus came out of the water, the Holy Spirit came down from heaven like a dove. God's voice called, "You are my son. I love you. I am pleased with you."

A Day in the Life of Jesus

Matthew–Mark
Luke–John

Jesus prayed to his father.
Jesus helped others. Jesus was kind.

Jesus taught people about God.
Jesus loved little children. Jesus was happy.

Jesus told a woman about living water.
Jesus healed a man who came through the roof.
Jesus talked to Zacchaeus.

Then Jesus went out in a boat to rest.

Jesus Calms the Storm

Matthew 8

One day Jesus went for a boat ride with his friends
who were called disciples.

The day was bright and sunny. The water was calm.

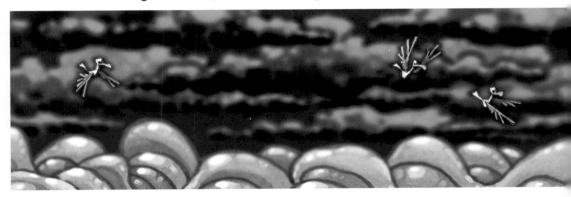

Suddenly a storm blew across the lake. The sky became dark.

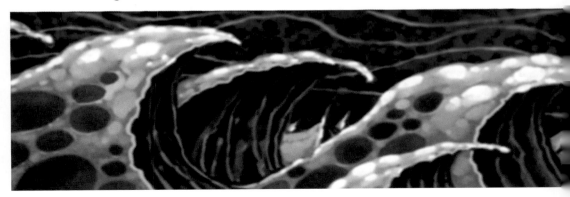

The water was choppy. The waves grew **bigger** and **bigger**.

The disciples were terrified. They hung onto the boat as the waves tossed it up and down. Jesus was sound asleep.

"Jesus, wake up!" the disciples shouted.
"The storm is scary. We are going to die!"

Jesus calmly stood up in the boat and looked at the storm.

"Be still," Jesus called out to the wind and the waves.

The wind stopped blowing. The waves calmed down.
The sun came out.

"Wow," thought the disciples. "Jesus is really special. Even the wind and the waves do what he says."

The Good Samaritan

Luke 10:25–27

"Who is my neighbor?" a man asked Jesus.
Jesus told him this story.

A man was traveling along the road from Jerusalem
to Jericho when bad guys attacked him.

The bad guys knocked him down.

They grabbed his hat and coat. They took his staff and all his money. They threw him in a ditch and walked away.

A priest came down the road, looked at the man, and walked past him.

A Levite traveled by, saw the man, and walked away.

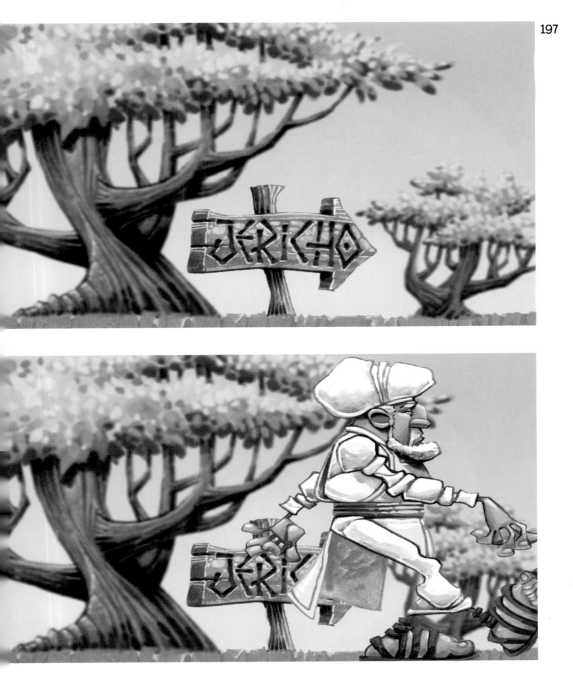

Then a Samaritan came along.
He saw the man and felt sorry for him.

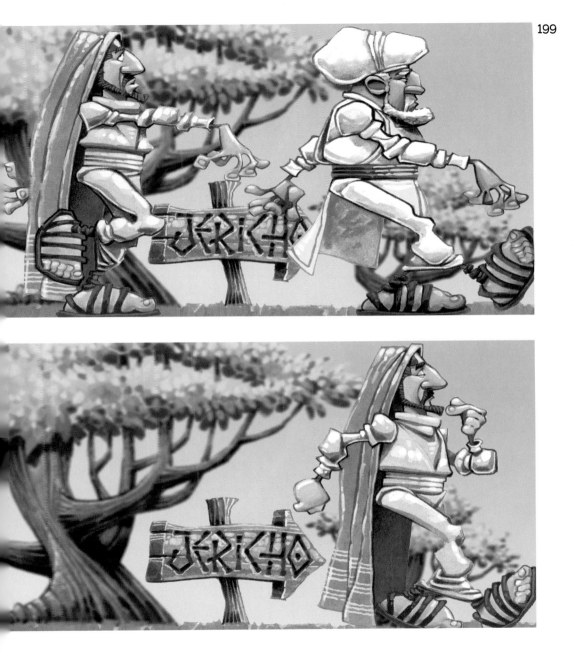

The Samaritan stopped to help. He cleaned the man's wounds and put bandages on them. He took good care of the man. The Samaritan was the only one who was a good neighbor.

The Lost Sheep

Luke 15:1-10

Jesus told a story about a man who had 100 sheep.

The shepherd carefully counted his sheep and lambs:
1—2—3—4, up to 99.

When he got to 100, there were no more sheep!
There were no more lambs. Number 100 was missing!

The shepherd spent all day looking for Little Lamb 100.

He looked up and down. He whistled.

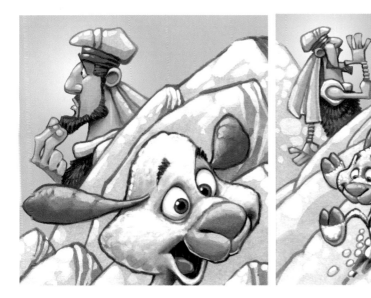

Where did that lamb go?   He called.

But Little Lamb 100 did not listen. He did not come.

Evening came. The night was dark. Little Lamb 100 was worried.

He missed his home. He missed the shepherd.
He heard strange noises that scared him.

Suddenly Little Lamb 100 saw the friendly shepherd.
He ran to him squealing with joy.
"Welcome home, Little Lamb 100," the shepherd said.

"Look who I found," said the shepherd. "Little Lamb 100 is back safe and sound." Every sheep and every lamb from Number 1 to Number 99 rejoiced.

The Ten Lepers

Luke 17:11–19

Ten men lived outside a village in a field. They had a bad skin disease and stayed away from other people.

One day Jesus visited their field.
"Jesus," the men called out. "Please heal us."

"Go to the temple and show yourselves
to the priests," Jesus told them.

The ten men headed for the temple. On their way they realized their sores were gone and their skin was clear. Jesus had healed them!

"HOORAY! We are well again!"
The ten men shouted.

Nine men ran away, but one remembered Jesus.

The man turned around and met Jesus on the road.
"Thank you, Jesus," he said. "You healed me."

The Lost Son

Luke 15:11-32

Jesus told a story about a father and his son.

One day the son said to his father, "Father, give me my
allowance. I want to get away from this farm and go to the city."

The father gave his son a lot of money.
"Be wise. Be careful," the father said.

"Bye, Dad," the son yelled.
And he headed off to the big city.

The son was not wise. He was not careful. He gave his new friends his money and invited them to big parties. He spent his money quickly.

Suddenly his money was all gone... and
his friends were gone too.

The son had no money. He needed a job.
He headed for a pig farm to take care of the pigs.

The pigs ate well, but the son was hungry. "I'm going home,"
the son said. "The workers on my dad's farm eat well. Maybe if I say
I'm sorry, Dad will let me work for him."

The son carefully approached his father's farm.
The father saw his son coming.

The father ran out to meet his son, jumping for joy.
"You've come home!" he shouted. "WELCOME BACK!"

"I'm sorry, Dad," the son said.
"Oh, my son, you are forgiven," the father said. "You were lost, and now you are home again. It's time to celebrate!"

Jesus and the Children

Mark 10:13-16

The children watched Jesus as they played.

Come over here, Jesus signaled to them.

The children ran to Jesus.

They jumped on his lap. They laughed with joy.

Jesus was happy to be with them.
Jesus loves all the children of the world.

Jesus Dies

Mark 14-15

Jesus prayed to God while he knelt
in the Garden of Gethsemane.

In the middle of the night, Judas
and a crowd of people entered the garden.

The men arrested Jesus and marched him to Jerusalem.

The soldiers put a crown of thorns on Jesus' head.
They whipped him.

Jesus carried a heavy cross to a hill named Golgotha.

The soldiers put Jesus on a cross to die.

After Jesus died, his friends took his body down
from the cross. They wrapped his body in cloth.

Joseph of Arimathea carried Jesus' body away ...

... and laid it in a tomb.

Joseph and the women rolled a big stone in front of the
tomb. They were very sad that Jesus was dead.

Soldiers stood in front of the tomb
to guard Jesus' body.

Jesus' work was done.
He died to save us from our sins.

Jesus Lives Again

Matthew 28

The soldiers guarding Jesus' tomb were scared.
Something strange had happened.

An angel came down from heaven.
He moved the stone away from the tomb.

Early in the morning, Jesus' friends came to the tomb.
"Who rolled the stone away?" they asked.

"What happened to Jesus?"

The angel said to them, "Jesus is not here. He has come back to life. Go and tell the others."
The women turned around and saw Jesus. They were very surprised and happy to see Jesus alive again.

A Miracle Catch of Fish

John 21

Early one morning Jesus stood on the shore of the Sea of Galilee. "How is the fishing?" Jesus called to his disciples. "Did you catch any fish?"

"No," the disciples called back.
"We fished all night, but our net is empty."

"Throw your net in the water on the right side of the boat," Jesus said. "Then you will catch some fish."

The disciples did what Jesus said. They threw the net back in the water on the other side of the boat.

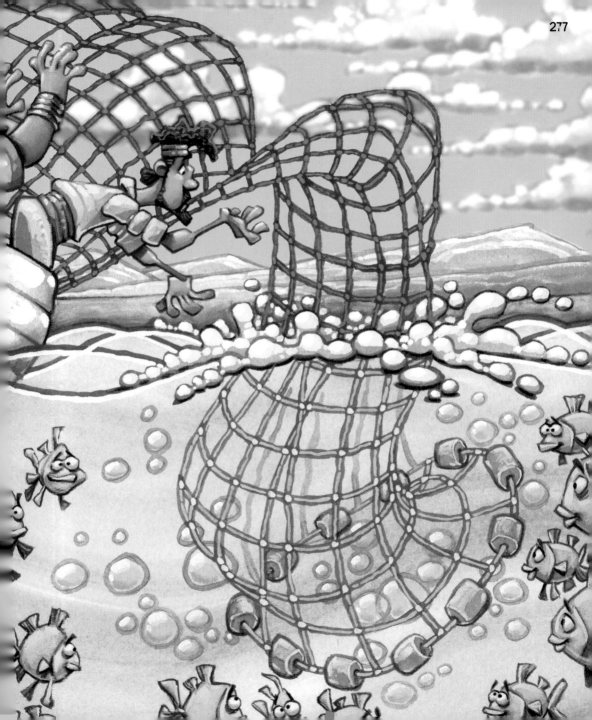

Fish swam into the net and filled it up.
This was a miracle! The disciples struggled to pull
the net full of fish to shore.

Jesus cooked some of the fish for their breakfast on the beach.
The disciples listened to everything Jesus said.
They were happy to be with Jesus again.

Jesus Goes to Heaven

Acts 1

"I can't stay with you anymore," Jesus said to his disciples. "But don't worry. I will send the Holy Spirit to be with you. Then you will be ready to tell the world about me."

Suddenly Jesus was lifted up toward heaven.

HIGHER ...

and HIGHER ... and HIGHER.

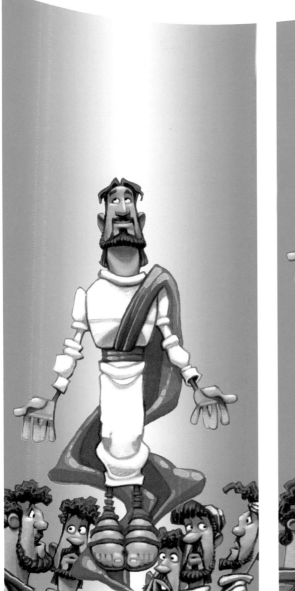